ED EMBERLEY'S
GREAT THUMBPRINT DRAWING BOOK

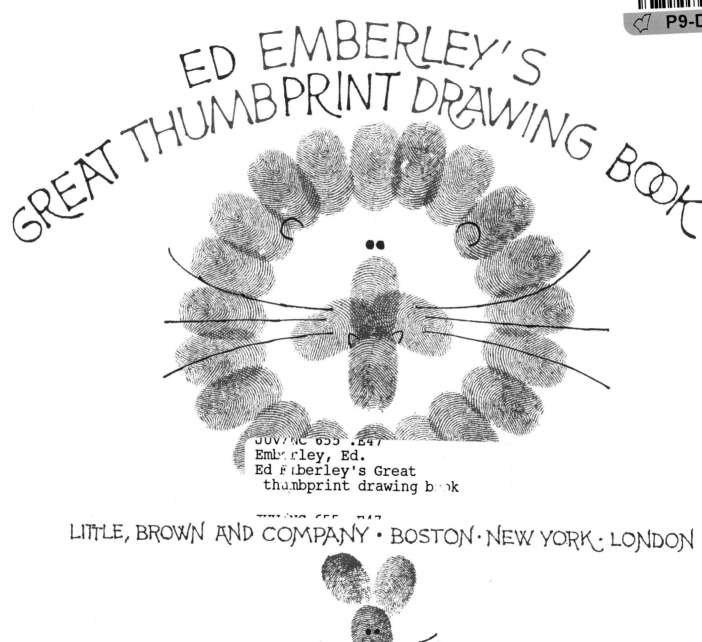

LITTLE, BROWN AND COMPANY · BOSTON · NEW YORK · LONDON

20 19

LIBRARY OF CONGRESS CATALOGING IN PUBLICATION DATA
EMBERLEY, ED.
    ED EMBERLEY'S GREAT THUMBPRINT DRAWING BOOK.

    SUMMARY: INSTRUCTIONS FOR CREATING A VARIETY OF SHAPES
AND FIGURES USING THUMBPRINTS AND A FEW SIMPLE LINES.
    1. THUMBPRINTS IN ART—JUVENILE LITERATURE.   2. DRAWING—
INSTRUCTION— JUVENILE LITERATURE.
    [1. THUMBPRINTS IN ART. 2. DRAWING—INSTRUCTION]   I. TITLE.
II. TITLE: GREAT THUMBPRINT DRAWING BOOK.

NC 655. E47   760'. 028   76-57346
ISBN 0·316-23613-6

PRINTED IN THE UNITED STATES OF AMERICA   WOR

OTHER DRAWING BOOKS BY ED EMBERLEY:
        ED EMBERLEY'S DRAWING BOOK OF ANIMALS
        ED EMBERLEY'S DRAWING BOOK OF FACES
        ED EMBERLEY'S DRAWING BOOK, MAKE A WORLD

WHERE TO FIND IT PAGE

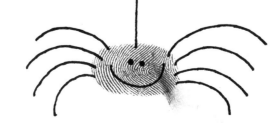

THIS BOOK SHOWS HOW TO DRAW PICTURES.
USING THIS NAME AND THUMBPRINTS.

iVY LOU

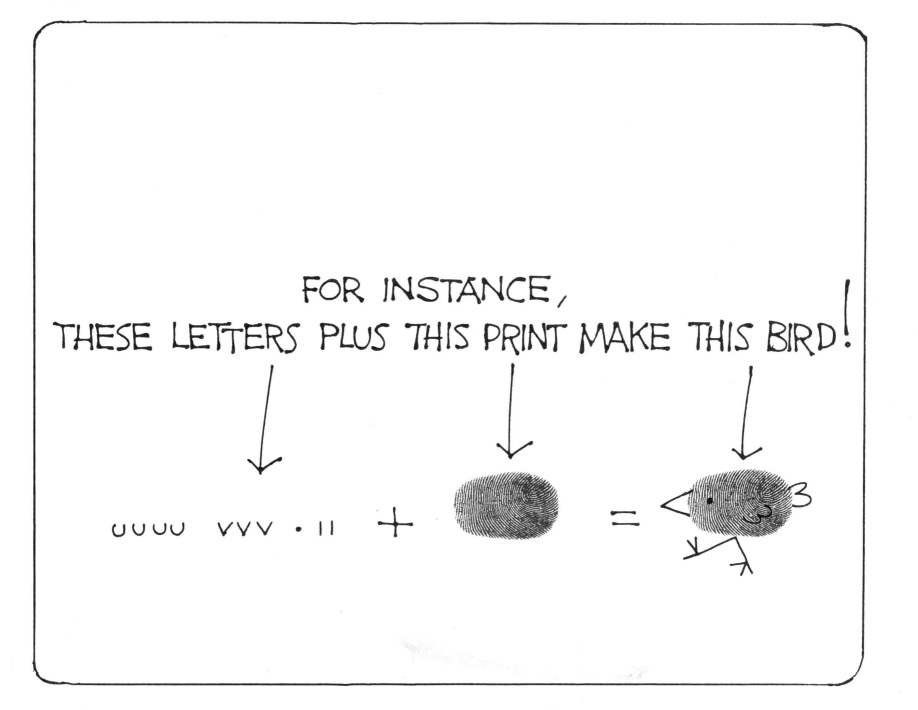

HERE'S HOW

THIS ROW SHOWS
WHAT TO DRAW.

THIS ROW SHOWS
WHERE TO PUT IT.

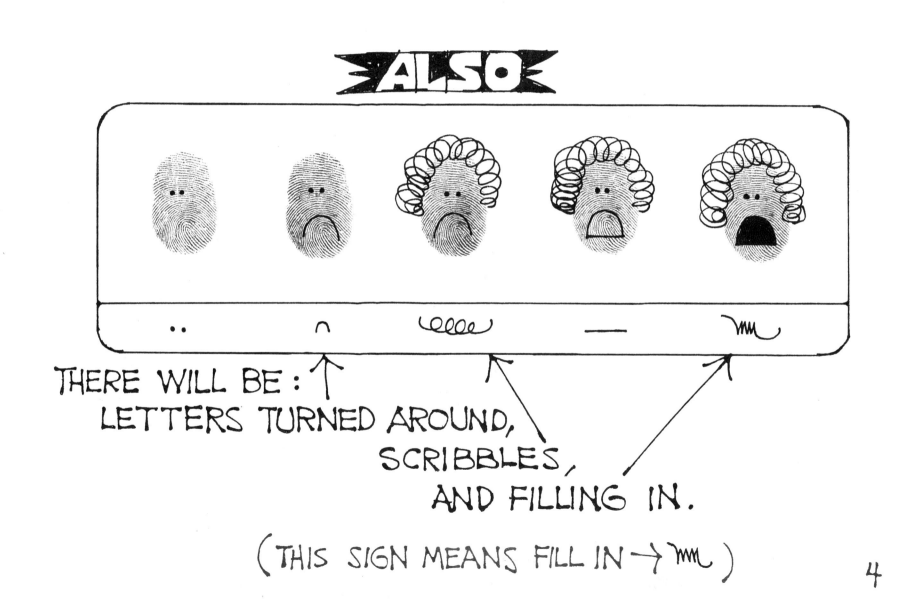

4

FOR INSTANCE

PERSON (MORE FOLKS ON PAGE 9)

(JUST A LINE CAN MAKE A HAT.)

WALKING (MORE ACTION ON PAGE 15)

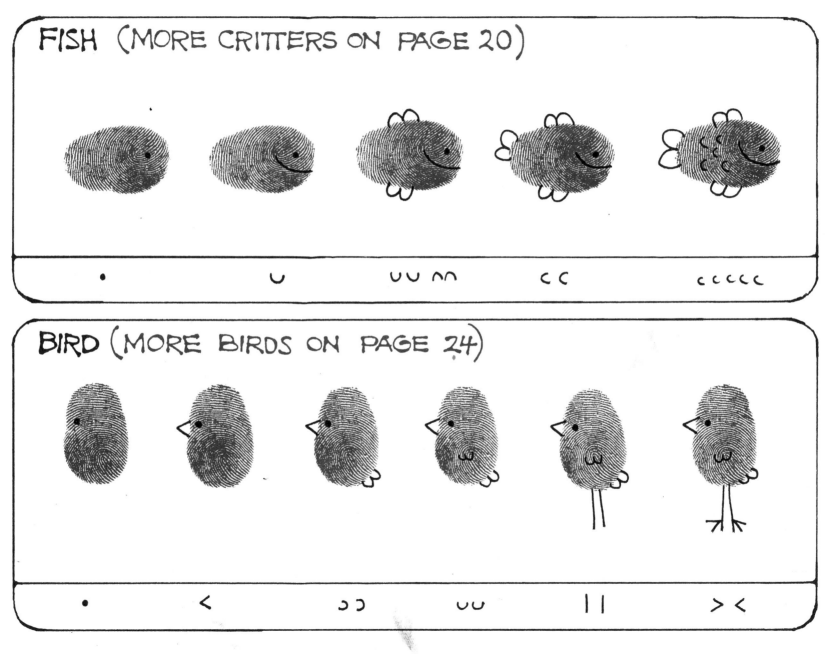

FISH (MORE CRITTERS ON PAGE 20)

BIRD (MORE BIRDS ON PAGE 24)

SPIDER (MORE BUGS ON PAGE 23)

RABBIT (MORE ANIMALS ON PAGE 20)

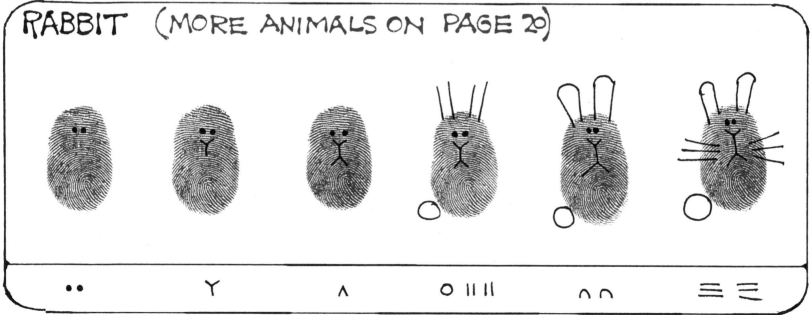

HALLOWEEN (MORE HOLIDAYS ON PAGE 26)

— ∧   ∧ ∧   ∧   — — —   ∪ ⋀⋀⋁

FROG (MORE THINGS WITH 2 THUMBPRINTS ON PAGE 31)

∩∩   ⌣   ●● .. |||| ∪∪ ∪∪

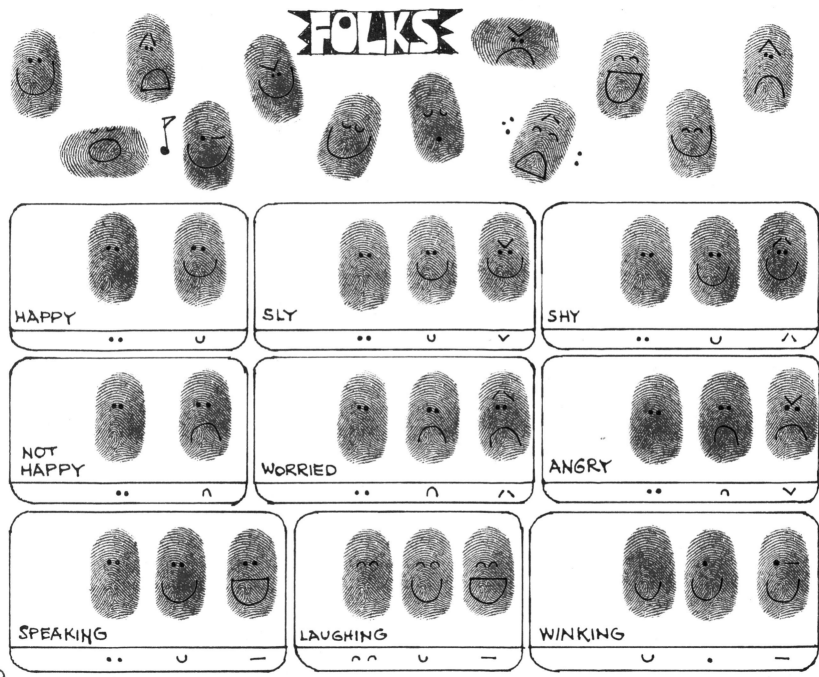

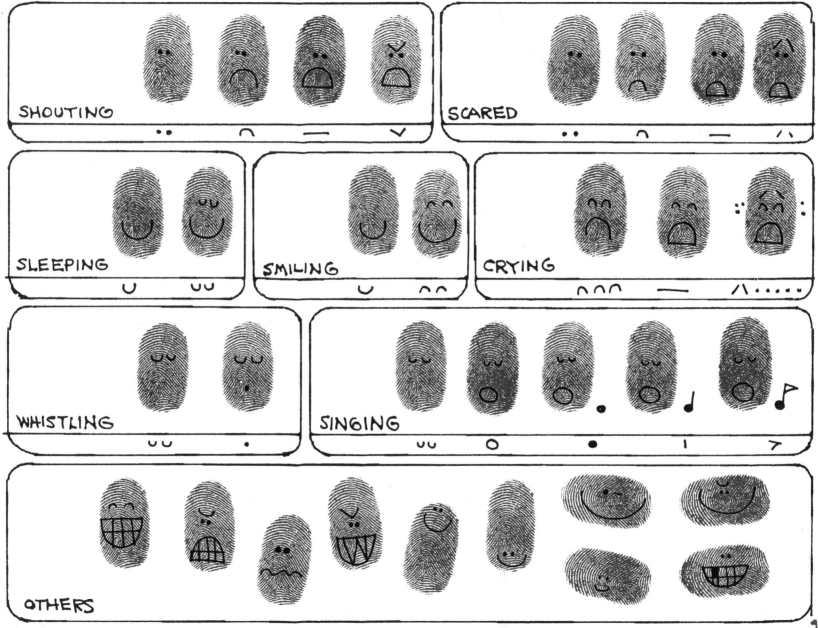

SHOUTING

SCARED

SLEEPING

SMILING

CRYING

WHISTLING

SINGING

OTHERS

10

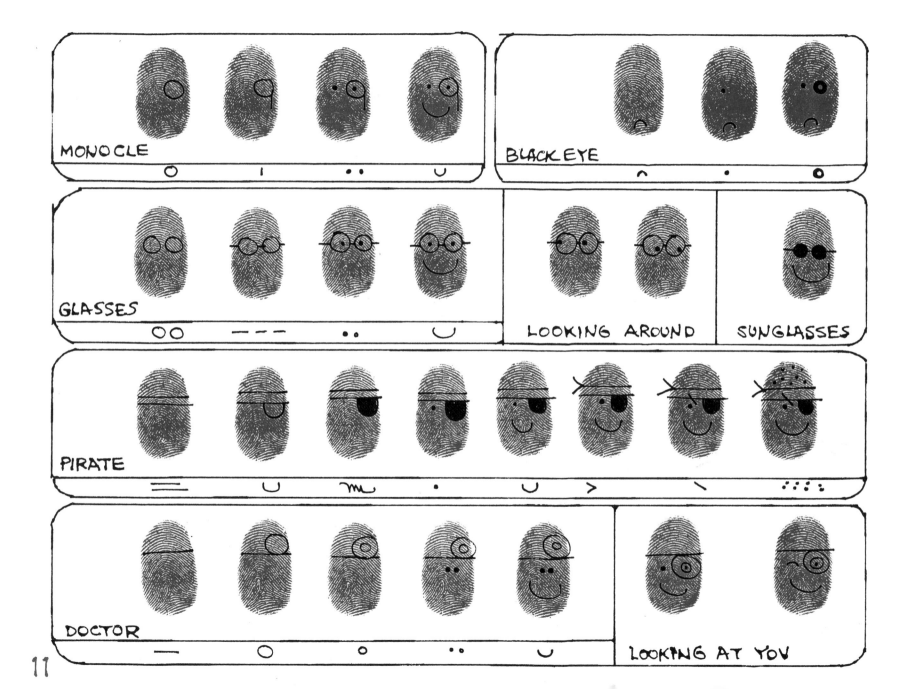

MONOCLE

BLACK EYE

GLASSES

LOOKING AROUND

SUNGLASSES

PIRATE

DOCTOR

LOOKING AT YOU

11

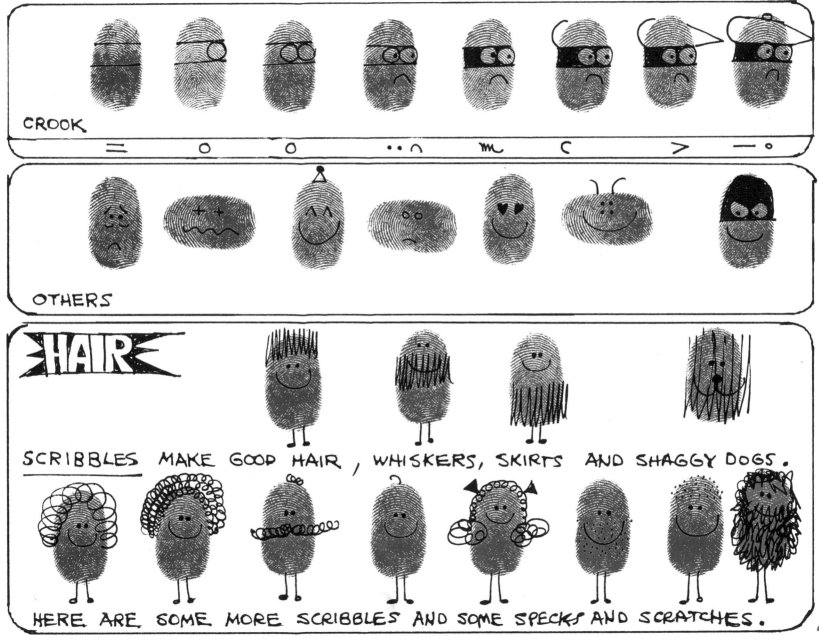

CROOK

OTHERS

HAIR

SCRIBBLES MAKE GOOD HAIR, WHISKERS, SKIRTS AND SHAGGY DOGS.

HERE ARE SOME MORE SCRIBBLES AND SOME SPECKS AND SCRATCHES.

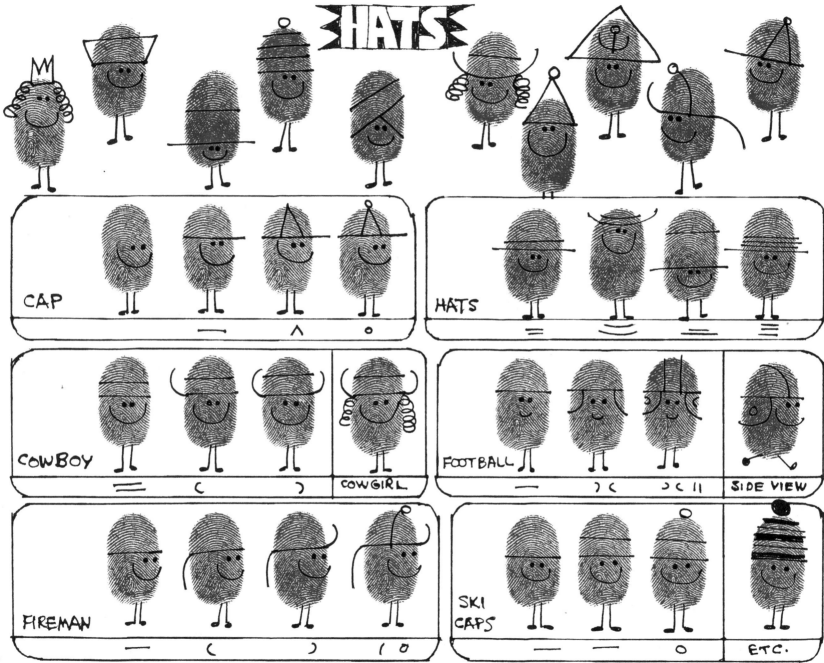

HATS

CAP

HATS

COWBOY — COWGIRL

FOOTBALL — SIDE VIEW

FIREMAN

SKI CAPS — ETC.

13

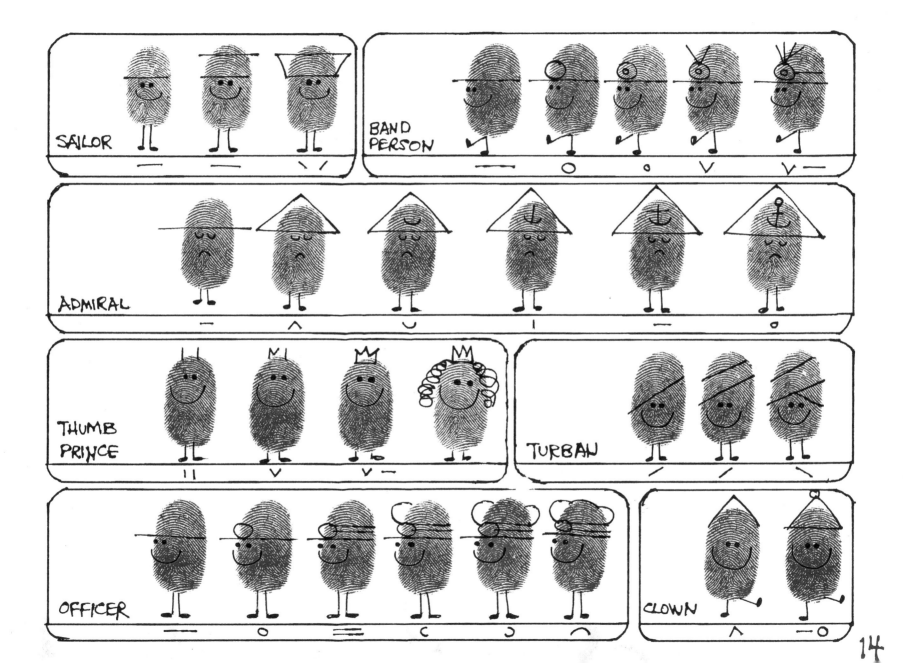

SAILOR

BAND PERSON

ADMIRAL

THUMB PRINCE

TURBAN

OFFICER

CLOWN

14

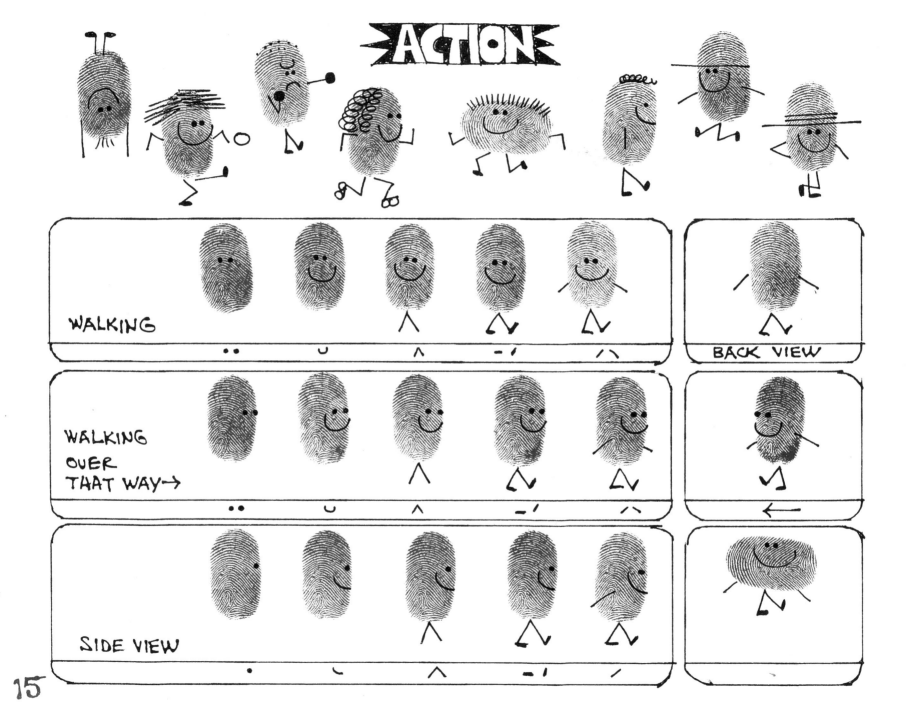

ACTION

WALKING

.. ‿ ^ ‑⁄ ‿

BACK VIEW

WALKING OVER THAT WAY →

.. ‿ ^ ‑⁄ ‿

←

SIDE VIEW

. ‿ ^ ‑⁄ ⁄

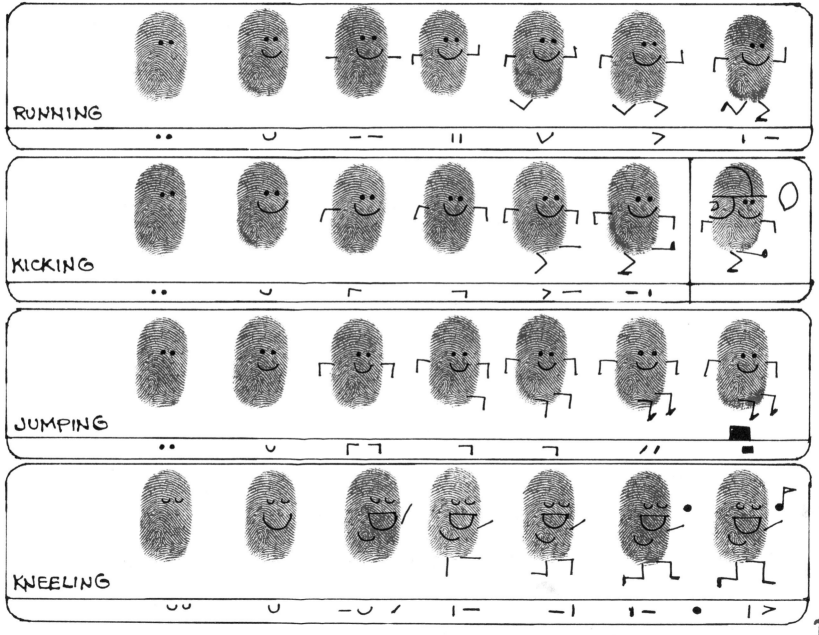

RUNNING

KICKING

JUMPING

KNEELING

16

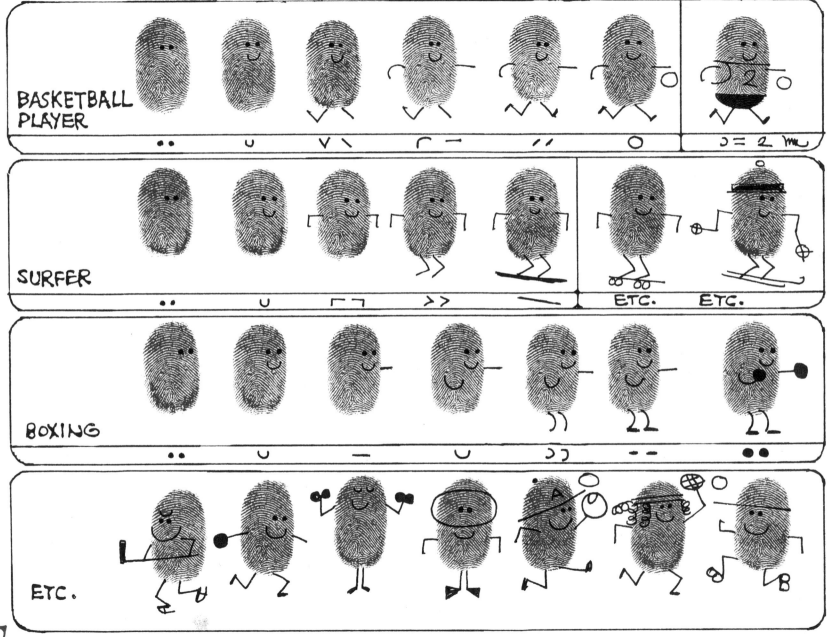

BASKETBALL PLAYER

SURFER   ETC.   ETC.

BOXING

ETC.

17

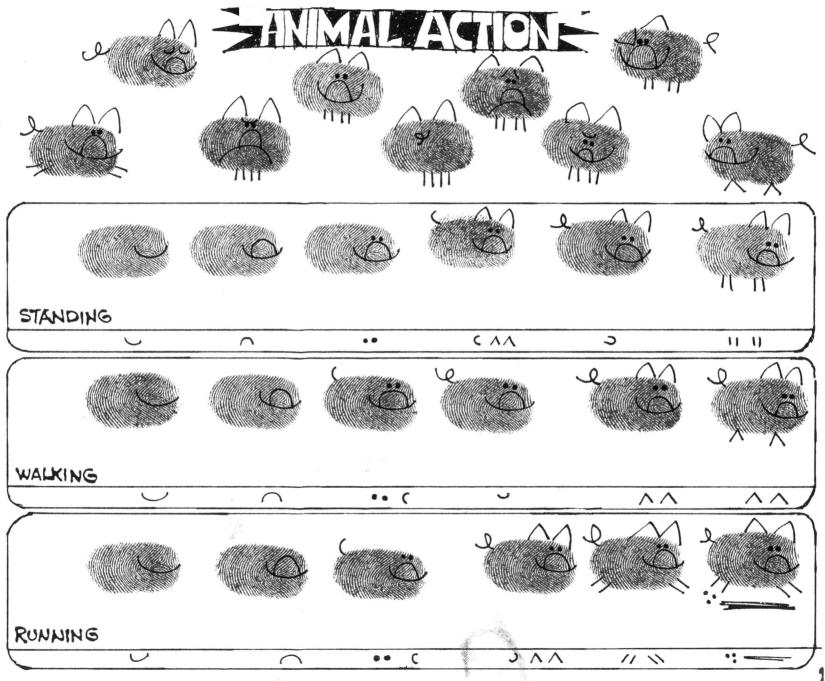

ANIMAL ACTION

STANDING

WALKING

RUNNING

18

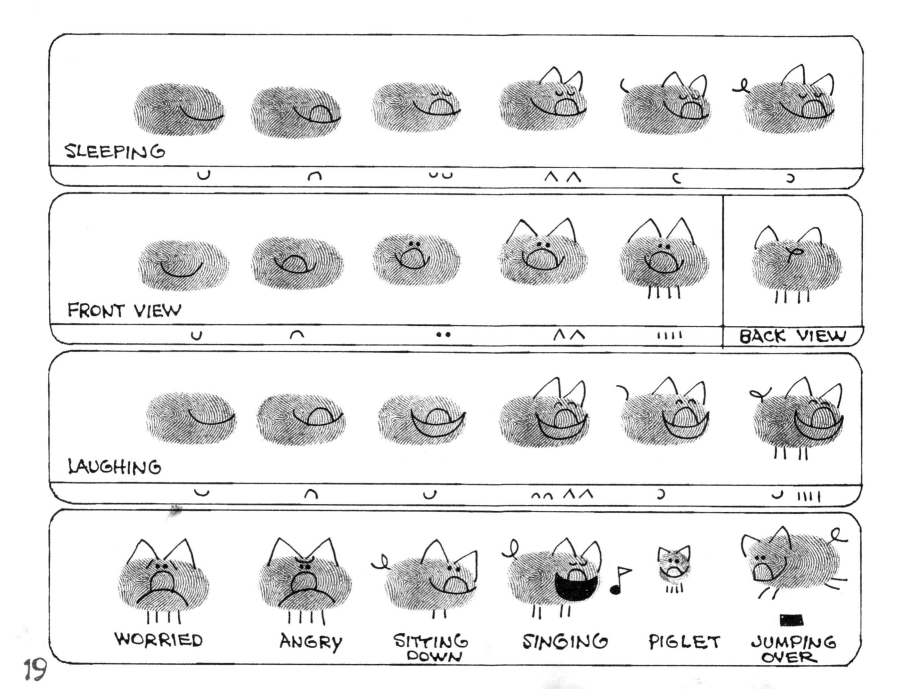

SLEEPING

FRONT VIEW

BACK VIEW

LAUGHING

WORRIED   ANGRY   SITTING DOWN   SINGING   PIGLET   JUMPING OVER

19

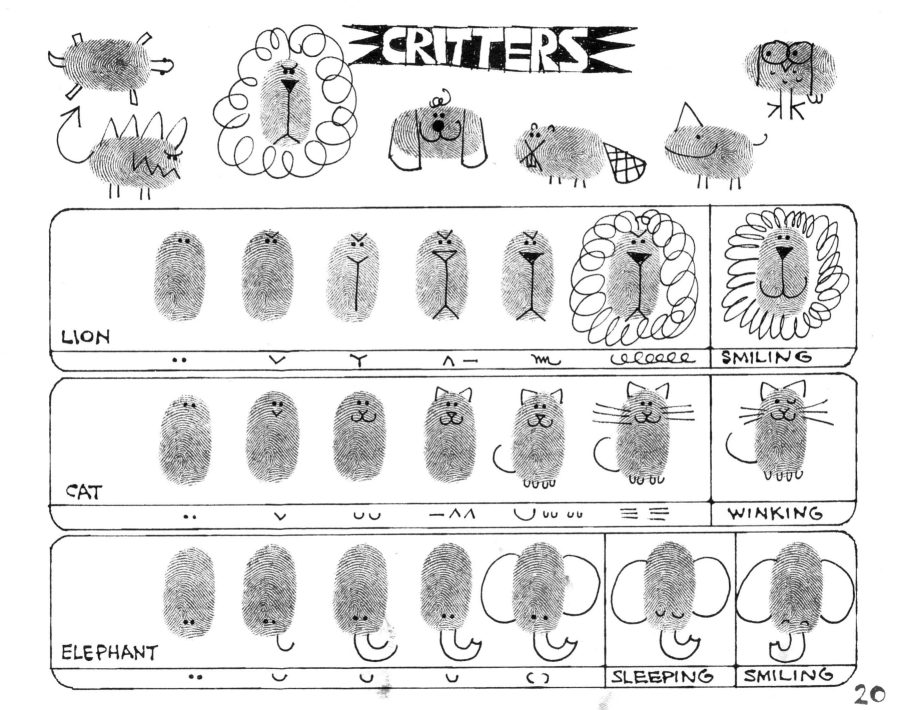

CRITTERS

LION   ..   ∨   Y   ∧ —   ᵚᵚᵚ   ℓℓℓℓℓ   SMILING

CAT   ..   ∨   ∪∪   —∧∧   ∪ ∪∪ ∪∪   ≡ ≡   WINKING

ELEPHANT   ..   ∪   ∪   ∪   ()   SLEEPING   SMILING

20

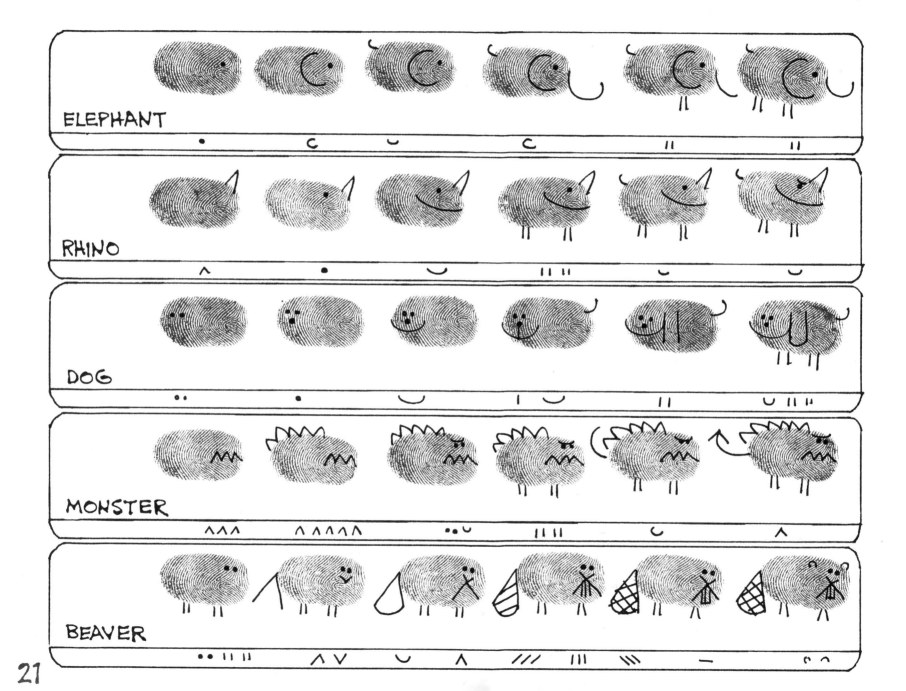

ELEPHANT

RHINO

DOG

MONSTER

BEAVER

21

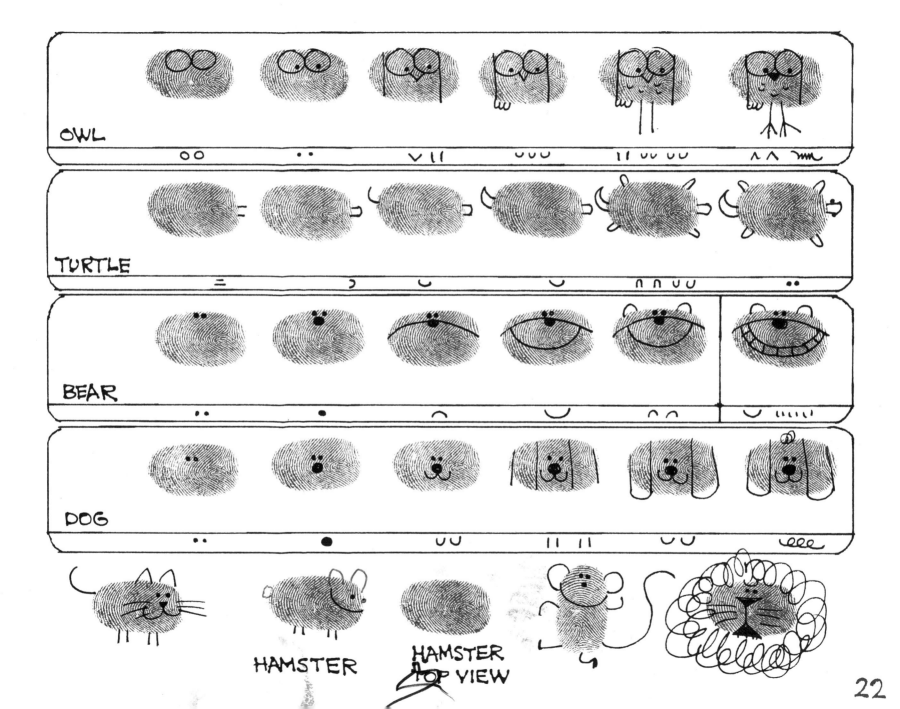

OWL

TURTLE

BEAR

DOG

HAMSTER

HAMSTER TOP VIEW

22

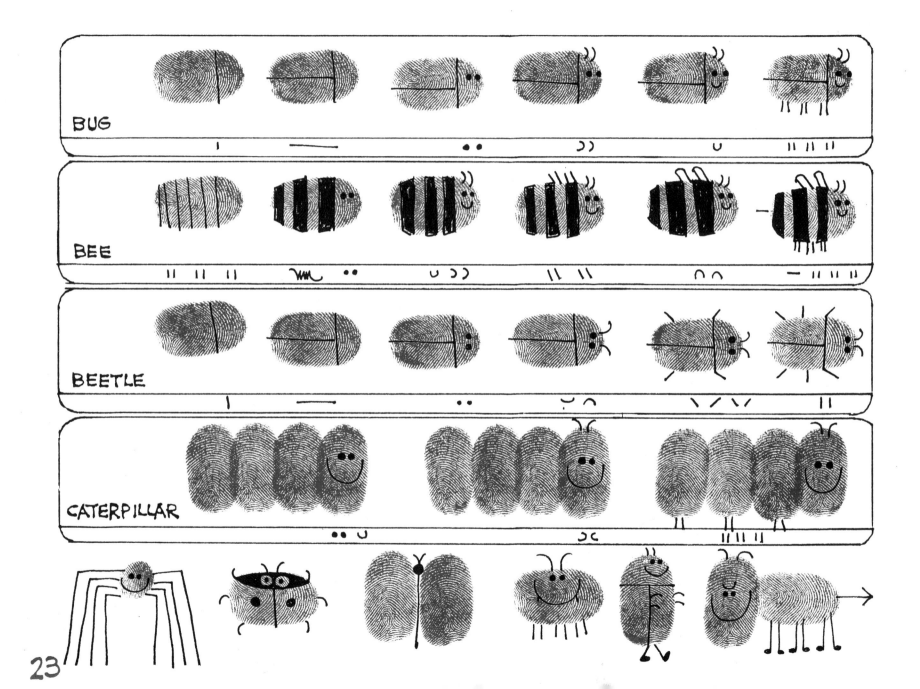

BUG

BEE

BEETLE

CATERPILLAR

23

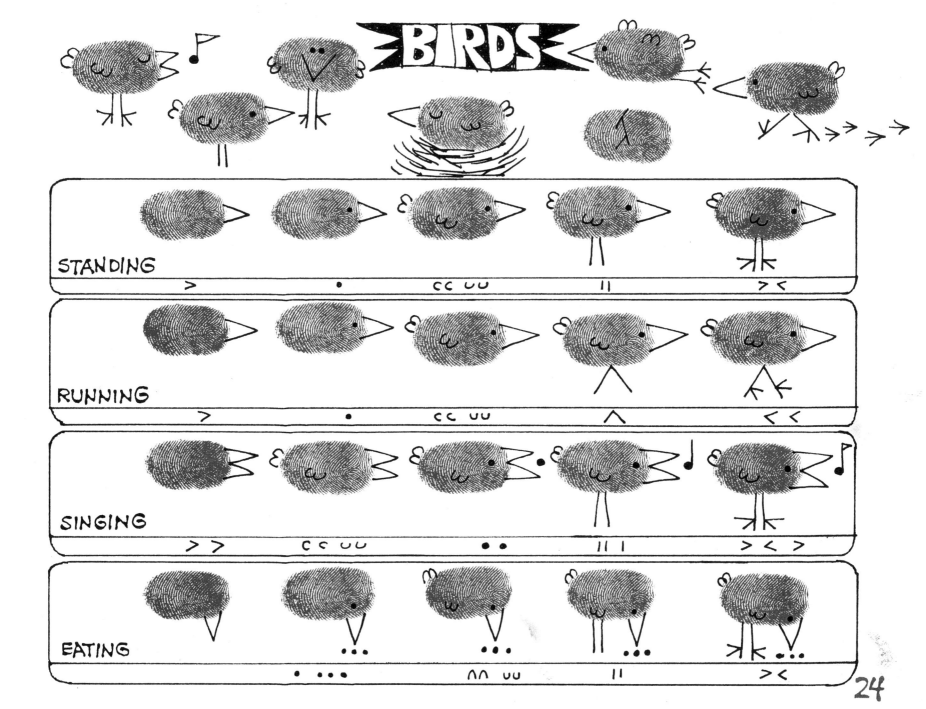

BIRDS

STANDING

RUNNING

SINGING

EATING

24

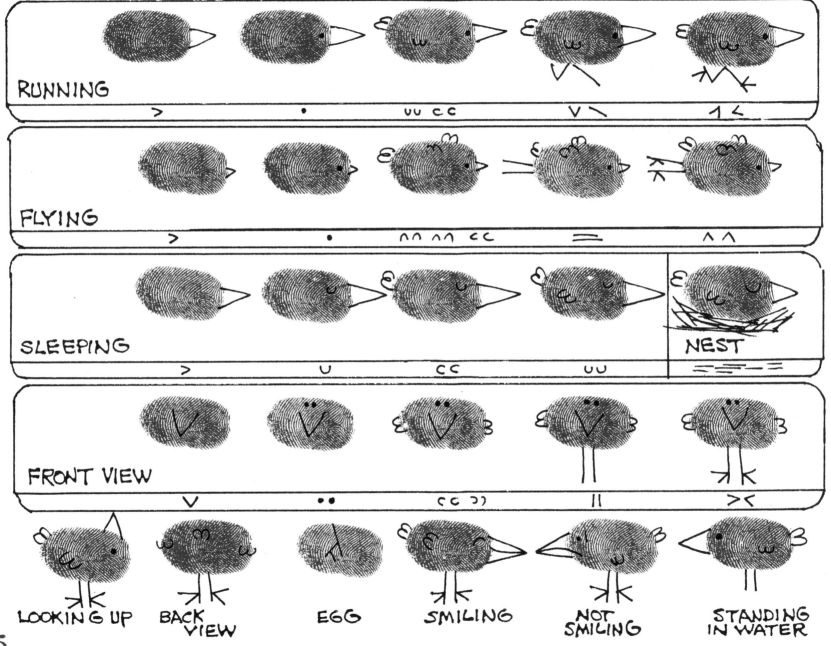

RUNNING

> · ∪∪ cc ∨\ ↑↙

FLYING

> · ∩∩ ∩∩ cc = ∧ ∧

SLEEPING

NEST

> ∪ cc ∪∪ ═══

FRONT VIEW

∨ •• cc ɔɔ ‖ ><

LOOKING UP   BACK VIEW   EGG   SMILING   NOT SMILING   STANDING IN WATER

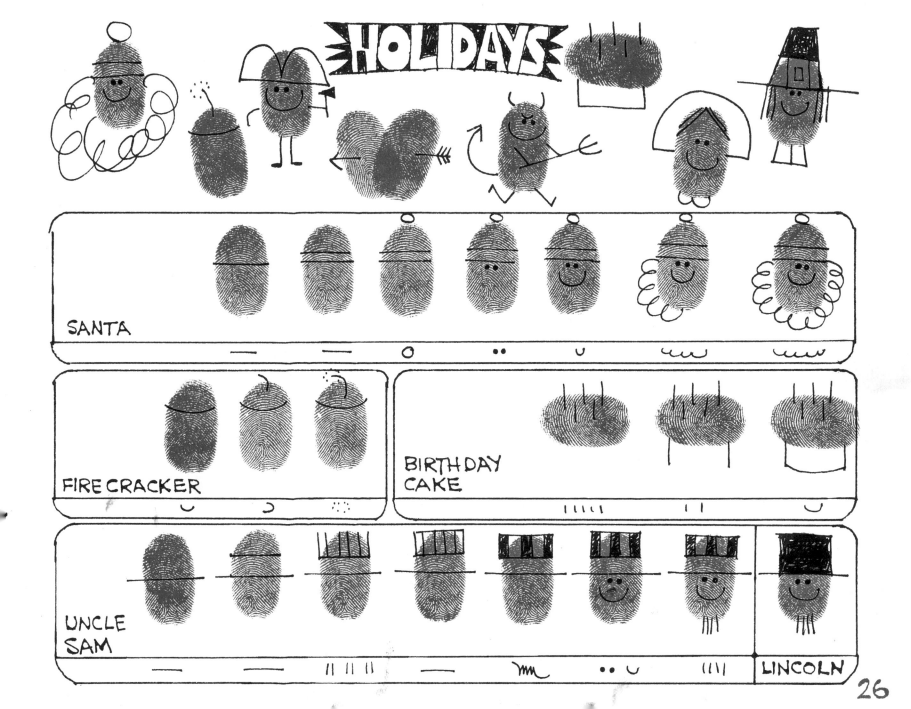

HOLIDAYS

SANTA

FIRE CRACKER

BIRTHDAY CAKE

UNCLE SAM

LINCOLN

26

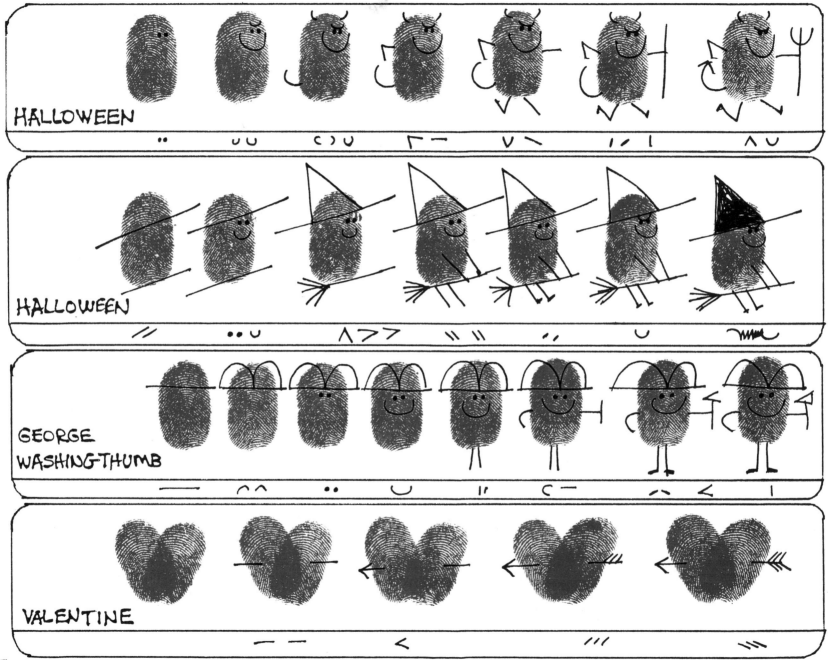

HALLOWEEN

HALLOWEEN

GEORGE
WASHING-THUMB

VALENTINE

27

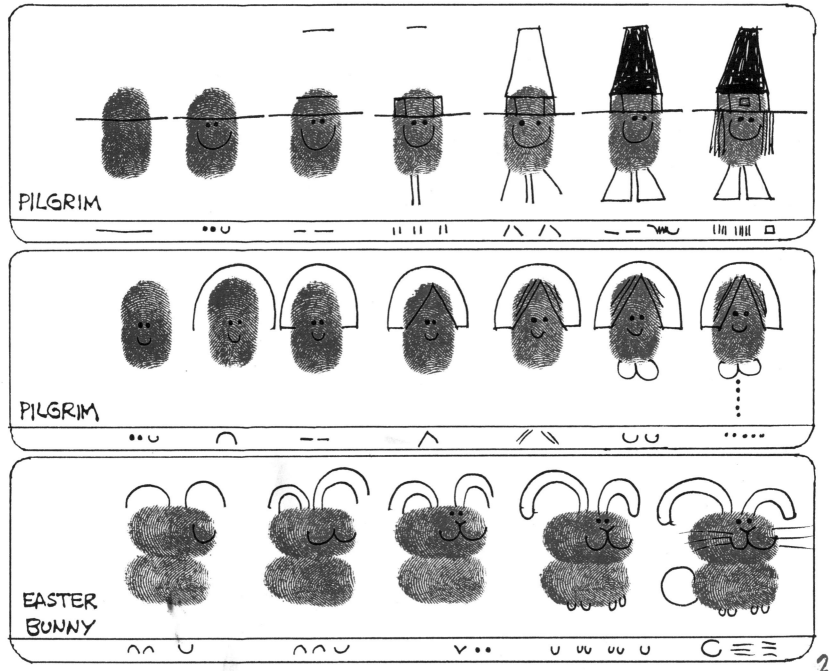

PILGRIM

PILGRIM

EASTER
BUNNY

28

FLOWERS

29

30

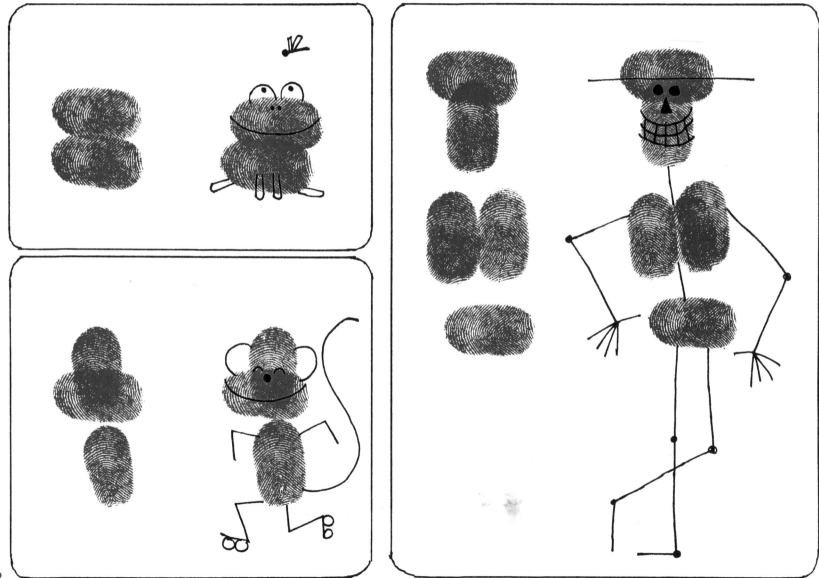

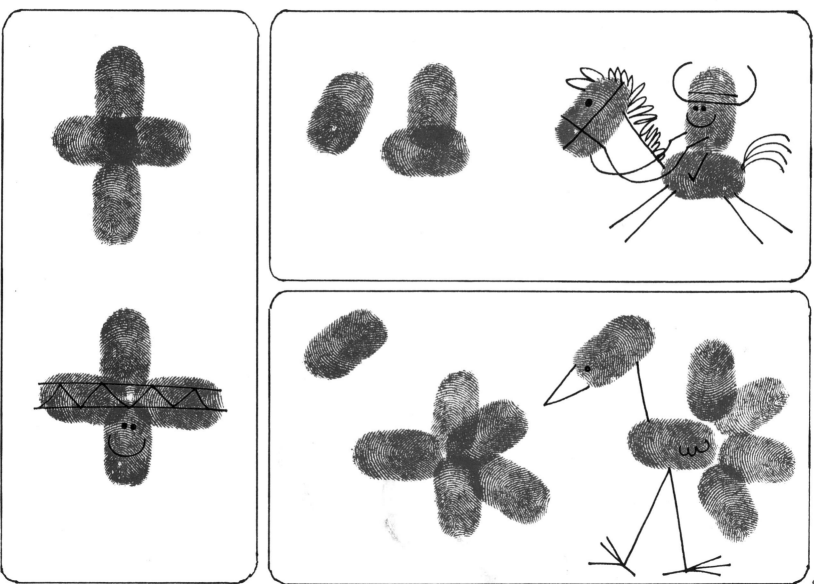

32

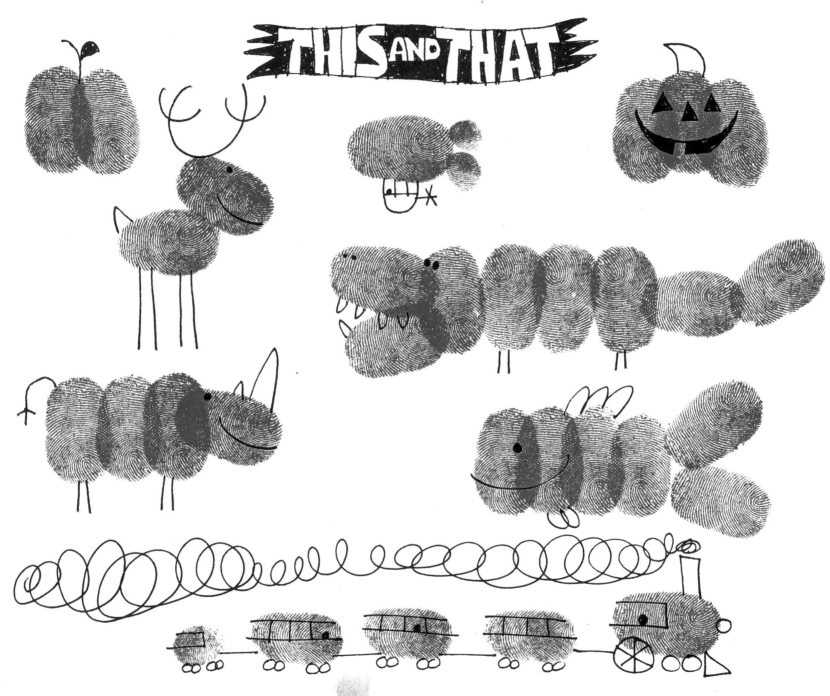

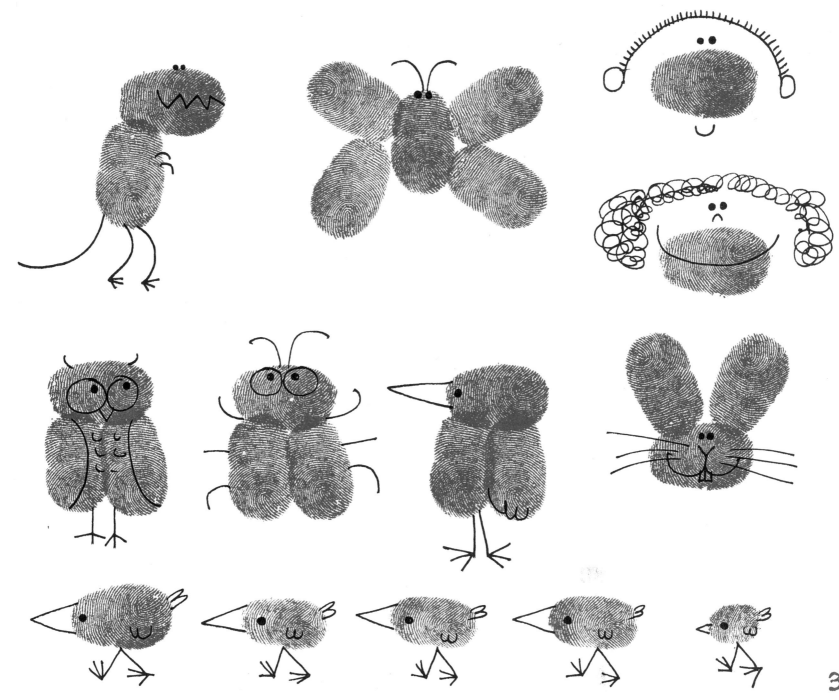

34

FOR THIS BOOK I USED A STAMP PAD I BOUGHT IN THE 5 AND 10.

A METAL BOX.

A DAMP, INKY SPONGE INSIDE.

I PRESSED MY THUMB ON THE PAD.

THEN I PRESSED MY THUMB ON THE PAPER —

I LET THE PRINT DRY—

THEN I DREW ON IT.

YOU CAN PAINT YOUR THUMB WITH WATER COLOR OR POSTER PAINT AND STAMP IT.

POSTER PAINT

YOU CAN MAKE YOUR OWN PAD FROM A SPONGE OR A FOLDED CLOTH SOAKED WITH FROSTING COLOR.

YOU CAN USE A CUT CARROT OR POTATO.

CUT   PAINT   STAMP   DRY   DRAW

YOU CAN DRAW A ROUND SHAPE OR MAKE A BLOB.

BLOB   ROUND SHAPE   PAINTED THUMB   STAMP PAD   CARROT   POTATO

- THERE ARE MORE THAN
  4 BILLION THUMBS
  IN THIS WORLD.
- NO TWO THUMBPRINTS
  HAVE <u>EVER</u> BEEN FOUND
  THAT ARE JUST ALIKE.
- THAT MEANS THAT THERE
  IS NO OTHER THUMBPRINT
  IN THIS WORLD EXACTLY LIKE YOURS.
- I THINK THAT MAKES YOUR THUMBPRINT SOMETHING SPECIAL!

Ed Emberley

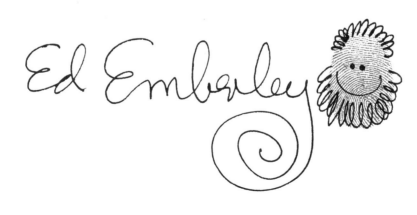